ABOUT THE AUTHOR:

Jenna Clake's debut collection, *Fortune Cookie*, was awarded the Melita Hume Prize and shortlisted for a Somerset Maugham Award. In 2018, she received an Eric Gregory Award from the Society of Authors.

BY THE SAME AUTHOR:

Fortune Cookie (Eyewear, 2017)

ACKNOWLEDGEMENTS:

Many thanks to the College of Arts and Law at the University of Birmingham for awarding me funding to write these and other poems, to Luke Kennard for his guidance, to Stuart Bartholomew for his kindness, enthusiasm, and support. With love to my family, who will never buy me anything red.

CLAKE/ Interview for is #2 in our Experimental Pamphlet Series following on from Luke Kennard's *Truffle Hound* (Sep, 2018).

CLAKE

Jenna Clake

VERVE
POETRY PRESS
BIRMINGHAM

PUBLISHED BY VERVE POETRY PRESS
Birmingham, West Midlands, UK
www.vervepoetrypress.com
mail@vervepoetrypress.com

FIRST PUBLISHED OCT 2018

Printed in Birmingham by Positive Print

ISBN: 978-1-912565-10-8

CONTENTS

When your boyfriend is away, listen to
podcasts all day, every day.

Clake's boyfriend left this morning without saying goodbye. Clake doesn't know when he is coming back, or where he has gone. She can only just bring herself to open the doors to the garden. She is sitting on the doorstep. Clake is so sad she has a headache over her right eye. She guesses that the red roses will bloom in three days, the white ones in seven.

Clake cuts off all her hair. She cuts it short. Her skin is red from where she has been scratching. Clake looks at herself every time she cuts into another chunk. She thinks, *This doesn't feel like anything.* She has always wanted to dye her hair blue. Clake usually cuts Boyfriend's hair. Boyfriend always has to fold his ears down and Clake nearly always accidentally jabs Boyfriend in the head. She hasn't ever made him bleed, though. Clake's cat doesn't know where Boyfriend is, and is meowing.

Clake bakes a cake. She says this over and over in her head while she stirs the mixture. It could become a tongue-twister children say in the playground. She is playing loud music but she can still hear her neighbour slamming their front door. She heard their washing machine earlier, and it reminded her of her mother. Clake has made Boyfriend's favourite as an apology. She has written SORRY on top of the cake in red icing.

Spiders have started coming into the house. At first, Clake lets her cat kill them, but after a while, she feels sorry for them. She traps them underneath plastic cups and places a post-it on each one saying SPIDER, just in case she forgets what is under there. Clake's cat hides under the duvet all day in protest. Before she places a cup over it, a spider says, *Please, we didn't mean to*. While Clake lies in bed, she can hear the spiders whispering to each other.

When they first moved into the house, Clake and Boyfriend barely spent any time here. They were always out. Clake wonders if Boyfriend is bored of their life. Clake's cat says, *You are thinking too much. Go to sleep.*

One of Boyfriend's friends has uploaded a photo of him asleep on a bench in the sun. Clake takes the cushions from the sofa and puts them on the floor. She copies Boyfriend's position, and pretends she is lying next to him.

Clake's eyelashes are falling out more than usual. Whenever she finds one of Boyfriend's, she tells him to make a wish. Clake has been wishing on her eyelashes. She wishes, every time, that Boyfriend will come home soon. Clake asks her cat, *If you make the same wish on multiple eyelashes, does it reverse the first wish?* Clake's cat says, *My eyelashes are different to yours. I don't know.*

Clake dreams that she and boyfriend are in a strange city. They are walking down a road. They pass an iron gate with gloves placed on the decorative spikes. There is a sign underneath the gloves saying: GLOVE SPEED DATING. There are phone numbers written on it. Boyfriend takes out a pen and writes Clake's number.

Clake has been clumsy today. She has hit her head on the doorframe, trapped her thumb between the bathroom door handle and the lock, hit her ankle on the leg of a chair. Eventually, Clake sits in the middle of the living room, wrapped in a duvet. The ceiling cracks.

Clake's cat has gone missing. Over the past two days, Clake has taught her to come to the sound of a bag of treats being shaken. Clake is proud of herself; Boyfriend hasn't been able to do that. Today, Clake's cat won't return. Clake has checked behind all the trees and usual hiding spots. She wants to call Boyfriend and cry. Clake has just printed fifty LOST CAT posters to put around the streets. Clake turns around and finds her cat on the windowsill.

Clake dreams that she and Boyfriend have returned to her university to watch a play by a Drama society. Clake loses Boyfriend and cannot find him. Her teeth are moving in her gums. She sees an old friend, who wants advice on eating disorders. Clake says to her old friend: *I thought it would be impossible to lose him.* When Clake finds Boyfriend, the performance has already started, and Boyfriend is angry with her for interrupting the actors. Clake argues with two people on the door until they allow her to leave. Clake and Boyfriend are staying in a hotel. Boyfriend comes back very drunk, and Clake puts him in the shower to cool down. She takes off her clothes and joins him. Boyfriend has brought another girl home and she joins them in the shower. Boyfriend kisses the girl and grabs her breasts.

Clake's cat is waiting for Boyfriend on the windowsill. Clake wonders if her cat knows that he will be home today. Clake has spent the morning cleaning the house. She scrubbed a stain in the carpet for one hour. It looks a little lighter. Clake falls asleep on the sofa. It is a dreamless sleep, and when she wakes up, Clake's cat is asleep on her feet. Clake's cat is dreaming; her whiskers twitch and she moves her back paws. Clake thinks, *I hope she is catching spiders in her dreams.* When she wakes up, Clake's cat says, *I was dreaming that Boyfriend brought another woman home. I felt like we should leave.* Clake turns on the TV and does not move from the sofa all night.

Clake has nearly eaten all of the cake she baked for Boyfriend. It was going stale. She fed whole pieces to her cat. Clake's cat licked the buttercream, and then gave up. Each time she has cut a slice, Clake has re-written SORRY so that Boyfriend will be able to see the whole word no matter which slice he gets. On the last slice she has written: SORRY SORRY SORRY SORRY SORRY SORRY SORRY SORRY SORRY SORRY.

The red roses have bloomed. Clake says to her cat, *I should let the spiders go.* Clake carries the spiders outside one by one and tips them out of their cups into the grass. Clake's cat chases, but doesn't hurt them. After they have done this, they finish the cake to celebrate. The white rose bush has more buds, and Clake rethinks that part of her prediction. Clake turns to her cat: *Do you want Boyfriend to come back?* Clake's cat twitches her ears.

ABOUT VERVE POETRY PRESS

Verve Poetry Press is a new press focussing initially on meeting a local need in Birmingham - a need for the vibrant poetry scene here in Brum to find a way to present itself to the poetry world via publication. Co-founded by Stuart Bartholomew and Amerah Saleh, it will be publishing poets this year from all corners of the city - poets that represent the city's varied and energetic qualities and will communicate its many poetic stories.

As well as publishing wonderful collections from poets with local links, such as Casey Bailey, Nafeesa Hamid, Leon Priestnall, Rupinder Kaur and Polarbear, we will also work with other people who have close connections to our sister festival, Verve. Our Experimental Pamphlet Series, our poetry show collection from Matt Abbott and our anthology with Lunar Poetry Podcasts all fall on this side of our activity.

Like the festival, we will strive to think about poetry in inclusive ways and embrace the multiplicity of approaches towards this glorious art.

So watch this space. Verve Poetry Press has arrived!

www.vervepoetrypress.com
@VervePoetryPres
mail@vervepoetrypress.com

Interview for

Jenna Clake

VERVE
POETRY PRESS
BIRMINGHAM

CONTENTS

Interview for an interviewer, a woman's voice, a voiceover and a Google Car driver

[A drone flies over a park, capturing three children cheering on a dog as it chases a squirrel. The dog becomes bored of the squirrel, chews a twig. The children become bored of the dog, play on the swings.]

VOICEOVER:
At what point did you think this would be helpful?

[A woman is being interviewed. She has chosen to remain anonymous, so only her silhouette can be seen.]

WOMAN:
We didn't really understand what we were doing. They told us we could sleep for as long as we wanted, so we did. I may have lost three years; no one is actually sure.

INTERVIEWER [off-camera]:
You are extraordinary!

VOICEOVER:
The woman was asleep for three months. Doctors are conducting a secret experiment.

[A statement appears on the screen: *No drones were harmed in the making of this documentary. We have used the DJI Phantom 4 model at all times.*]

VOICEOVER:
Today, we are following one of Google's Street View cars.

[A drone follows a black car on the motorway. The car changes lanes frequently. The drone flies in through the open passenger-side window of the car and lands on the seat. The driver looks at the drone.]

DRIVER:
We are driving to Bristol today. We prefer to take pictures on sunny days, but it is overcast. We will be photographing all the residential roads in the Montpelier area. That's Saint Andrew's Road, Fairlawn Road, Cobourg Road, Lower Cheltenham Place, Albany Road, Brook Road, Albert Park Place, Banner Road, Shaftesbury Avenue, Wellington Avenue, Picton Street, Picton Lane, Bath Buildings, Richmond Road and York Road. If I have time, I might go to Clifton. I like it when you catch someone unaware in the window, or in their front garden. It makes it look friendlier. Most of the pictures look so sad and empty, like no one lives there.

[The drone flies out of the passenger window and follows the car for the rest of the journey.]

*

[The woman cries.]

WOMAN:
A producer has just told me the truth: I lost fifteen years. They have taken the mirrors out of my flat so I can't hurt myself when I get back.

INTERVIEWER [off-camera]:
You are beautiful!

[The woman leans forward.]

WOMAN:
Let me tell you something.

[The drone is flying around the park. It is being chased by the dog. The dog is barking. The children look up from their picnic. The drone flies closer to the children.]

WOMAN:
And that's all I have to say.

[The Google driver does not capture a person in their window, or front garden. The drone flies away. The Google driver waves.]

Interview for a woman's voice, a man's voice and a voiceover (1)

[The man is holding an umbrella (bright red).]

WOMAN:
That is not your umbrella.

MAN:
When I was a child, I thought if it rained enough, sharks would appear in the puddles.

WOMAN:
How did they get in the sea to begin with?

VOICEOVER:
When a glove is dropped into a puddle, it looks like a dead spider.

MAN:
It will stop raining at seven minutes past four.

[A gust of wind moves the woman's skirt (bright red). She smooths it down.]

VOICEOVER:
In an art gallery, metal buckets collect rain. Each bucket holds dozens of goldfish. The fish nibble skin.

WOMAN:
Do you ever think about your first kiss?

[The man's hair is soaked. Drops of rain hang on his eyelashes.]

Interview for a woman's voice and a voiceover (1)

[The kitchen. All the appliances are bright red.]

WOMAN:
The moment I open something, I have to buy another.

VOICEOVER:
The woman does not know that her clock has been losing one hour every week.

WOMAN:
When I was younger, my mother gave me a bottle of Barbie perfume. I wore it every day – dabbed it behind my ears like she did. I always thought her ears were so delicate: they curved like a single feather.

[The fridge whirs.]

VOICEOVER:
The woman is colour-blind.

WOMAN:
I didn't know that it would run out eventually.

[The woman takes plates from the drying rack and places them in a bowl of soapy water.]

WOMAN:
An unopened packet makes me feel like I have another chance.

Interview for a woman's voice and a voiceover (2)

[The woman sits in bed (bright red).]

WOMAN:
A palm-reader refused to read my hand.

VOICEOVER:
As a child, the woman couldn't print her hands onto paper with paint. She liked to watch it dry in the cracks and lines of her skin.

[The woman looks at her right palm.]

WOMAN:
The palm reader walked me to the entrance and shut the door behind me like we'd had an argument.

[The woman takes out a small sewing kit and chooses a reel of cotton (bright red). The woman stiches through the top layer of skin on her left palm.]

Interview for a woman's voice and a voiceover (3)

[Members of the public take off their sunglasses. The footage is then played in reverse – the people put their sunglasses on again. This is repeated four times.]

VOICE OVER:
Everyone is always wearing a mask.

[A room (white); the woman is sitting in a chair (bright red).]

WOMAN:
I realised that wearing sunglasses when I walked to the train station made me feel safer; like every time I got cat-called, it wasn't so much of a violation because they couldn't see my eyes.

VOICE OVER:
You could say it's empowering.

WOMAN:
It isn't empowering, really. Not at all.

[The woman dives into a public swimming pool fully dressed. When she emerges, she wipes her eyes, smudging her make-up. The footage is reversed so that the woman jumps from the water and stands on the side, as dry as a new tissue. This is repeated four times.]

Interview for another woman's voice

ANOTHER WOMAN:
It got to the point where I could hear them through the walls.

[The man and the woman sit on a red sofa, facing forwards. They are on separate cushions.]

ANOTHER WOMAN:
It started two months ago.

[Another woman takes a glass and places it against the wall.]

ANOTHER WOMAN:
The phone is ringing.

[Another Woman presses on the base of the glass. As she pushes, the glass splinters.]

ANOTHER WOMAN:
I made a noise complaint.

[The man and the woman play a game of pat-a-cake.]

ANOTHER WOMAN:
When they got here, they said, 'There is nothing we can do about this.'

[The man hugs the woman. Her arms hang by her side.]

ANOTHER WOMAN:
They said, 'They have to work it out between themselves.'

[The woman hugs the man. His arms hand by his side. He looks like he has been put on a coat hanger.]

ANOTHER WOMAN:
The phone is ringing.

[The woman turns to the man.]

ANOTHER WOMAN:
I honestly don't know what to do.

Interview for a woman's voice and a voiceover (4)

VOICEOVER:
The woman decides to take a bath.

[The woman struggles to walk to the bathroom. She weeps as she pulls back the shower curtain (bright red).]

WOMAN:
I'm really sorry. I just don't feel well.

[The woman tests the water. It is lukewarm. She climbs into the bath, wearing her pyjamas (bright red).]

WOMAN:
I'm really sorry. I just don't feel well.

[The woman cries.]

VOICEOVER:
The woman has left the bathroom door open in case the man comes home to look after her.

WOMAN:
I'm really sorry. I just don't feel well.

VOICEOVER:
This is not an experiment. We wish we could tell her.

[The woman gets out of the bath and lies on the bed (bright red).]

Interview for a woman's voice, a man's voice and a voiceover (2)

[The man has built a copy of the house inside the house using mesh (bright red).]

VOICEOVER:
The woman has been trying to touch the balustrade.

MAN:
Don't touch anything.

VOICEOVER:
The light switches do not click.

[There is a white box around the mesh (bright red). The woman is only allowed to enter once she is naked.]

MAN:
You haven't been yourself recently.

[The man leaves the mesh house. He sets the alarm with the woman inside.]

WOMAN:
It's impossible to climb the stairs.

[The woman sleeps on the hallway floor.]

VOICEOVER:
The man has forgotten the game of hide and seek.

MAN:
You can come out when you feel more like yourself.

[The man staples the windows and doors shut.]

Interview for a woman's voice, a man's voice, and a voiceover (3)

[The man and the woman lie on the bedroom floor. They are wearing raincoats (bright red) and rain hats (bright red).]

VOICE OVER:
The rain will be coming soon.

[The woman takes off her shoes. They are like a little girl's school shoes.]

MAN:
The rain will be coming soon.

WOMAN:
I like to feel it with my toes.

MAN:
You are wearing socks.

VOICE OVER:
They are not doing right.

MAN:
How could you do this to me?

VOICE OVER:
Do it again with more emotion.

[The woman pushes her hair out of her eyes. The man unties and reties his scarf. The man and the woman roll to face each other. They look like they are trying to be teapots.]

WOMAN:
Do you have the umbrella?

MAN:
No.

WOMAN:
How could you do this to me?

VOICE OVER:
Do it again with more emotion.

[The woman rolls onto her back and lies like a dropped doll.]

WOMAN:
The rain will be coming soon.

Interview for a woman's voice and a voiceover (5)

[It is April, so it is raining.]

VOICEOVER:
The roof is still leaking.

[The woman catches the drips in a washing-up bowl (bright red).]

VOICEOVER:
No one answers.

[The woman empties the washing-up bowl (bright red) over the shrubs in the garden.]

WOMAN:
I have a pain in my ribs.

VOICEOVER:
It is keeping her awake at night.

[The woman cries over the washing-up bowl (bright red), then empties it over the shrubs in the garden.]

WOMAN:
The pain is starting to get worse. I'm sure that it is going to crack.

[The woman feels her rib. She discovers that a piece is missing.]

VOICEOVER:
The roof is leaking in a second place.

[The woman changes the position of the washing up bowl (bright red) every twelve hours. She places a tea towel (bright red) on the floor.]

WOMAN:
The gap in my rib is getting bigger.

[The woman measures the gap and writes the results on a piece of paper.]

WOMAN:
I was using mouthwash when I coughed up a piece of my rib.

VOICEOVER: It fell into the sink.

[The woman places the piece of her rib in a glass jar and holds it up to the light.]

VOICEOVER:
The roof is leaking in another place.

WOMAN:
I have a pain in another rib.

Interview for a woman's voice and a voiceover (6)

[The living room, without furniture. There is a large cube (bright red) in the centre of the room.]

VOICE OVER:
We have finally got through to her.

[The woman is lying down, on her side, in front of the cube.]

WOMAN:
I am so -

VOICE OVER:
We have finally got through to her.

WOMAN:
I am so -

[In the kitchen, everything that was not fixed down has gone.]

WOMAN:
I am so -

[The woman has poured white paint over the kitchen surfaces and cupboard doors.]

WOMAN:
I am so -

[The woman blinks.]

Interview for a woman's voice and herself

[The woman arrives home. She sees herself sitting on the stairs.]

HERSELF:
I believed the world would let me have things the right way.

[The woman shuts the curtains (bright red) as though hiding from something terrible.]

WOMAN:
You must acknowledge each thing you have lost out loud.

[Herself turns to look the woman in the eye.]

HERSELF:
[inaudible]

WOMAN:
You may forever think about one of those things and carry it with you.

[The woman and herself quickly close all the curtains (bright red). They leave.]

Interview for a presenter and voiceover

PRESENTER:
We have come here today, this greyed -

VOICEOVER:
- beach, to see a natural phenomenon -

PRESENTER:
[inaudible]

[The presenter is wearing a raincoat (bright red) and, around her neck, a seashell painted red and grey.]

PRESENTER:
It has been my life-long dream -

VOICE OVER:
Then they wheel it out. Who knows what makes -

PRESENTER:
- something so beautiful - [inaudible]

[A six-foot-tall seashell is wheeled out. The presenter is giddy.]

VOICE OVER:
The sea is violent and spraying the presenter. She does not make a sound.

PRESENTER:
[inaudible]

[The seashell has a large red tongue that lolls down its side.]

PRESENTER:
- not the red of lollipops, but the red of an acer tree. A strong -

VOICE OVER:
- scent of seaweed. We -

PRESENTER:
- must approach it carefully. We are -

VOICE OVER:
- certain of two things:

[The presenter takes a handful of -]

VOICE OVER:
- seashells out of her pockets; they are dry -

PRESENTER:
- even after hours – [inaudible]

[The seashell is happy to see them; it rolls its tongue to the other side.]

PRESENTER:
We are presenting it with an offering.

VOICE OVER:
The beach is getting greyer; the –

PRESENTER:
- movement of the tongue is one-hundred per cent involuntary.

[Meanwhile, the seashell is hatching a plan to escape.]

~